THE SPANISH CONSTITUTION

Passed by the Cortes Generales in Plenary Meetings of the Congress of Deputies and the Senate held on October 31, 1978

Ratified by the spanish people in the referendum of December 6, 1978

Sanctioned by His Majesty the King before the Cortes on December 27, 1978

Legibus, 2017

ISBN: 978-1978468566

Origen del documento: Agencia Estatal del Boletín Oficial del Estado

INDEX

PREAMBLE	4
PRELIMINARY TITTLE	4
PART I. *Fundamental Rights and Duties*	6
Chapter 1. Spaniards and Aliens	7
Chapter 2. Rights and Liberties	7
Division 1. Fundamental Rights and Public Liberties	8
Division 2. Rights and Duties of Citizens	12
Chapter 3. Principles governing Economic and Social Policy	14
Chapter 4. Guarantees of Fundamental Rights and Liberties	17
Chapter 5. Suspension of Rights and Liberties	17
PART II. *The Crown*	18
PART III. *The Cortes Generales (Parliament)*	21
Chapter 1. Houses of Parliament	21
Chapter 2. Drafting of Bills	26
Chapter 3. International Treaties	28
PART IV. *Government and Administration*	29
PART V. *Relations between the Government and the Cortes Generales*	32
PART VI. *Judicial Power*	34
PART VII. *Economy and Finance*	37
PART VIII. *Territorial Organization of the State*	41
Chapter 1. General Principles	41
Chapter 2. Local Government	41
Chapter 3. Self-governing Communities	42
PART IX. *The Constitutional Court*	50
PART X. *Constitutional Amendment*	53
ADDITIONAL PROVISIONS	54
TRANSITIONAL PROVISIONS	54
REPEALS	56
FINAL PROVISION	57

SPANISH CONSTITUTION

We, don Juan Carlos I, King of Spain, announce to all those who may have knowledge of this:
that the Cortes have passed and the Spanish people have ratified the following Constitution:

PREAMBLE

The Spanish Nation, desiring to establish justice, liberty, and security, and to promote the wellbeing of all its members, in the exercise of its sovereignty, proclaims its will to:
Guarantee democratic coexistence within the Constitution and the laws, in accordance with a fair economic and social order.
Consolidate a State of Law which ensures the rule of law as the expression of the popular will.
Protect all Spaniards and peoples of Spain in the exercise of human rights, of their culture and traditions, languages and institutions.
Promote the progress of culture and of the economy to ensure a dignified quality of life for all.
Establish an advanced democratic society, and
Cooperate in the strengthening of peaceful relations and effective cooperation among all the peoples of the earth.
Therefore, the Cortes pass and the Spanish people ratifies the following .

SPANISH CONSTITUTION

PRELIMINARY TITLE

Section 1

1. Spain is hereby established as a social and democratic State, subject to the rule of law, which advocates freedom, justice, equality and political pluralism as highest values of its legal system .
2. National sovereignty belongs to the Spanish people, from whom all state powers emanate.
3. The political form of the Spanish State is the Parliamentary Monarchy.

Section 2

The Constitution is based on the indissoluble unity of the Spanish Nation, the common and indivisible homeland of all Spaniards; it recognizes and guarantees the right to selfgovernment of the nationalities and regions of which it is composed and the solidarity among them all.

Section 3

1. Castilian is the official Spanish language of the State. All Spaniards have the duty to know it and the right to use it.
2. The other Spanish languages shall also be official in the respective Self-governing Communities in accordance with their Statutes.
3. The richness of the different linguistic modalities of Spain is a cultural heritage which shall be specially respected and protected.

Section 4

1. The flag of Spain consists of three horizontal stripes: red, yellow and red, the yellow strip being twice as wide as each red stripe.
2. The Statutes may recognize flags and ensigns of the Self-governing Communities. These shall be used together with the flag of Spain on their public buildings and in their official ceremonies.

Section 5

The capital of the State is the city of Madrid.

Section 6

Political parties are the expression of political pluralism, they contribute to the formation and expression of the will of the people and are an essential instrument for political participation. Their creation and the exercise of their activities are free in so far as they respect the Constitution and the law. Their internal structure and their functioning must be democratic.

Section 7

Trade unions and employers associations contribute to the defence and promotion of the economic and social interests which they represent. Their creation and the exercise of their activities shall be free in so far as they respect the Constitution and the law. Their internal structure and their functioning must be democratic.

Section 8

1. The mission of the Armed Forces, comprising the Army, the Navy and the Air Force, is to guarantee the sovereignty and independence of Spain and to defend its territorial integrity and the constitutional order.
2. The basic structure of military organization shall be regulated by an Organic Act in accordance with the principles of the present Constitution.

Section 9

1. Citizens and public authorities are bound by the Constitution and all other legal previsions.
2. It is the responsibility of the public authorities to promote conditions ensuring that freedom and equality of individuals and of the groups to which they belong are real and effective, to remove the obstacles preventing or hindering their full enjoyment, and to facilitate the participation of all citizens in political, economic, cultural and social life.
3. The Constitution guarantees the principle of legality, the hierarchy of legal provisions, the publicity of legal statutes, the non-retroactivity of punitive provisions that are not favourable to or restrictive of individual rights, the certainty that the rule of law shall prevail, the accountability of public authorities, and the prohibition of arbitrary action of public authorities.

PART I

Fundamental Rights and Duties

Section 10

1. The dignity of the person, the inviolable rights which are inherent, the free development of the personality, the respect for the law and for the rights of others are the foundation of political order and social peace.
2. Provisions relating to the fundamental rights and liberties recognized by the Constitution shall be construed in conformity with the Universal Declaration of Human Rights and international treaties and agreements thereon ratified by Spain.

CHAPTER 1

Spaniards and Aliens

Section 11

1. Spanish nationality shall be acquired, retained and lost in accordance with the provisions of the law.
2. No person of Spanish birth may be deprived of his or her nationality.
3. The State may negotiate dual nationality treaties with Latin-American countries or with those which have had or which have special links with Spain. In these countries Spaniards may become naturalized without losing their nationality of origin, even if those countries do not grant a reciprocal right to their own citizens.

Section 12

Spaniards come legally of age at eighteen years.

Section 13

1. Aliens in Spain shall enjoy the public freedoms guaranteed by the present Part, under the terms to be laid down by treaties and the law.

2. Only Spaniards shall have the rights recognized in section 23, except in cases which may be established by treaty or by law concerning the right to vote and the right to be elected in municipal elections, and subject to the principle of reciprocity. (This text includes the first constitutional reform adopted on 27/08/1992; it just added the words "and the right to be elected" to the paragraph).
3. Extradition shall be granted only in compliance with a treaty or with the law, on reciprocal basis. No extradition can be granted for political crimes; but acts of terrorism shall not be regarded as such.
4. The law shall lay down the terms under which citizens from other countries and stateless persons may enjoy the right to asylum in Spain.

CHAPTER 2

Rights and Freedoms

Section 14
Spaniards are equal before the law and may not in any way be discriminated against on account of birth, race, sex, religion, opinion or any other personal or social condition or circumstance.

DIVISION 1

Fundamental Rights and Public Freedoms

Section 15

Everyone has the right to life and to physical and moral integrity, and under no circumstances may be subjected to torture or to inhuman or degrading punishment or treatment. Death penalty is hereby abolished, except as provided for by military criminal law in times of war.

Section 16

1. Freedom of ideology, religion and worship of individuals and communities is guaranteed, with no other restriction on their expression than may be necessary to maintain public order as protected by law.
2. No one may be compelled to make statements regarding his or her ideology, religion or beliefs.
3. No religion shall have a state character. The public authorities shall take into account the religious beliefs of Spanish society and shall consequently maintain appropriate cooperation relations with the Catholic Church and other confessions.

Section 17

1. Every person has the right to freedom and security. No one may be deprived of his or her freedom except in accordance with the provisions of this section and in the cases and in the manner provided for by the law.
2. Preventive arrest may last no longer than the time strictly necessary in order to carry out the investigations aimed at establishing the events; in any case the person arrested must be set free or handed over to the judicial authorities within a maximum period of seventytwo hours.
3. Every person arrested must be informed immediately, and in a way understandable to him or her, of his or her rights and of the grounds for his or her arrest, and may not be compelled to make a statement. The arrested person shall be guaranteed the assistance of a lawyer during police and judicial proceedings, under the terms to be laid down by the law.
4. An habeas corpus procedure shall be provided for by law in order to ensure the immediate handing over to the judicial authorities of any person illegally arrested. Likewise, the maximum period of provisional imprisonment shall be determined by law.

Section 18

1. The right to honour, to personal and family privacy and to the own image is guaranteed.

2. The home is inviolable. No entry or search may be made without the consent of the householder or a legal warrant, except in cases of flagrante delicto.
3. Secrecy of communications is guaranteed, particularly regarding postal, telegraphic and telephonic communications, except in the event of a court order.
4. The law shall restrict the use of data processing in order to guarantee the honour and personal and family privacy of citizens and the full exercise of their rights.

Section 19

Spaniards have the right to freely choose their place of residence, and to freely move about within the national territory. Likewise, they have the right to freely enter and leave Spain subject to the conditions to be laid down by the law. This right may not be restricted for political or ideological reasons.

Section 20

1. The following rights are recognized and protected:
a) the right to freely express and spread thoughts, ideas and opinions through words, in writing or by any other means of reproduction.
b) the right to literary, artistic, scientific and technical production and creation.
c) the right to academic freedom.
d) the right to freely communicate or receive truthful information by any means of dissemination whatsoever. The law shall regulate the right to the clause of conscience and professional secrecy in the exercise of these freedoms.
2) The exercise of these rights may not be restricted by any form of prior censorship.
3. The law shall regulate the organization and parliamentary control of the masscommunication means under the control of the State or any public agency and shall guarantee access to such means by the significant social and political groups, respecting the pluralism of society and of the various languages of Spain.
4. These freedoms are limited by respect for the rights recognized in this Part, by the legal provisions implementing it, and especially by the right to honour, to privacy, to the own image and to the protection of youth and childhood.
5. The seizure of publications, recordings and other means of information may only be carried out by means of a court order.

Section 21

1. The right to peaceful unarmed assembly is granted. The exercise of this right shall not require prior authorization.

2. In the case of meetings in public places and of demonstrations, prior notification shall be given to the authorities, who can only forbid them when there are well founded grounds to expect a breach of public order, involving danger to persons or property.

Section 22

1. The right of association is granted.
2. Associations which pursue ends or use means legally defined as criminal offences are illegal.
3. Associations set up on the basis of this section must be entered in a register for the sole purpose of public knowledge.
4. Associations may only be dissolved or have their activities suspended by virtue of a court order stating the reasons for it.
5. Secret and paramilitary associations are prohibited.

Section 23

1. Citizens have the right to participate in public affairs, directly or through representatives freely elected in periodic elections by universal suffrage.
2. They also have the right to accede under conditions of equality to public functions and positions, in accordance with the requirements laid down by the law.

Section 24

1. All persons have the right to obtain effective protection from the judges and the courts in the exercise of their rights and legitimate interests, and in no case may there be a lack of defense.
2. Likewise, all have the right to the ordinary judge predetermined by law; to defense and assistance by a lawyer; to be informed of the charges brought against them; to a public trial without undue delays and with full guarantees; to the use of evidence appropriate to their defense; not to make self-incriminating statements; not to plead themselves guilty; and to be presumed innocent.
The law shall specify the cases in which, for reasons of family relationship or professional secrecy, it shall not be compulsory to make statements regarding allegedly criminal offences.

Section 25

1. No one may be convicted or sentenced for actions or omissions which when committed did not constitute a criminal offence, misdemeanour or administrative offence under the law then in force.
2. Punishments entailing imprisonment and security measures shall be aimed at reeducation and social rehabilitation and may not involve forced labour. The

person sentenced to prison shall enjoy, during the imprisonment, the fundamental rights contained in this Chapter except those expressly restricted by the content of the sentence, the purpose of the punishment and the penitentiary law. In any case, he or she shall be entitled to paid work and to the appropriate Social Security benefits, as well as to access to cultural opportunities and the overall development of his or her personality.
3. The Civil Administration may not impose penalties which directly of indirectly imply deprivation of freedom.

Section 26

Courts of Honour are prohibited within the framework of the Civil Administration and of professional organizations.

Section 27

1. Everyone has the right to education. Freedom of teaching is recognized.
2. Education shall aim at the full development of human personality with due respect for the democratic principles of coexistence and for basic rights and freedoms.
3. The public authorities guarantee the right of parents to ensure that their children receive religious and moral instruction in accordance with their own convictions.
4. Elementary education is compulsory and free.
5. The public authorities guarantee the right of all to education, through general education programming, with the effective participation of all sectors concerned and the setting-up of educational centres.
6. The right of individuals and legal entities to set up educational centres is recognized, provided they respect constitutional principles.
7. Teachers, parents and, when appropriate, pupils shall participate in the control and management of all centres supported by the Administration out of public funds, under the terms established by the law.
8. The public authorities shall inspect and standardize the educational system in order to ensure compliance with the laws.
9. The public authorities shall help the educational centres which meet the requirements established by the law.
10. The autonomy of Universities is recognized, under the terms established by the law.

Section 28

1. All have the right to freely join a trade union. The law may restrict or except the exercise of this right in the Armed Forces or Institutes or other bodies subject to military discipline, and shall lay down the special conditions of its exercise by civil servants. Trade union freedom includes the right to set up trade unions and to

join the union of one's choice, as well as the right of trade unions to form confederations and to found international trade union organizations, or to become members thereof. No one may be compelled to join a trade union.

2. The right of workers to strike in defence of their interests is recognized. The law governing the exercise of this right shall establish the safeguards necessary to ensure the maintenance of essential public services.

Section 29

1. All Spaniards shall have the right to individual and collective petition, in writing, in the manner and subject to the consequences to be laid down by law.

2. Members of the Armed Forces or Institutes or bodies subject to military discipline may only exercise this right individually and in accordance with statutory provisions relating to them.

DIVISION 2

Rights and Duties of Citizens

Section 30

1. Citizens have the right and the duty to defend Spain.

2. The law shall determine the military obligations of Spaniards and shall regulate, with all due guarantees, conscientious objection as well as other grounds for exemption from compulsory military service; it may also, when appropriate, impose a community service in place of military service.

3. A civilian service may be established with a view to accomplishing objectives of general interest.

4. The duties of citizens in the event of serious risk, catastrophe or public calamity may be regulated by law.

Section 31

1 Everyone shall contribute to sustain public expenditure according to their economic capacity, through a fair tax system based on the principles of equality and progressive taxation, which in no case shall be of a confiscatory scope.

2. Public expenditure shall make an equitable allocation of public resources, and its programming and execution shall comply with criteria of efficiency and economy.

3. Personal or property contributions for public purposes may only be imposed in accordance with the law.

Section 32

1. Man and woman have the right to marry with full legal equality.
2. The law shall make provision for the forms of marriage, the age and capacity for concluding it, the rights and duties of the spouses, the grounds for separation and dissolution, and their effects.

Section 33

1. The right to private property and inheritance is recognized.
2. The social function of these rights shall determine the limits of their content in accordance with the law.
3. No one may be deprived of his or her property and rights, except on justified grounds of public utility or social interest and with a proper compensation in accordance with the law.

Section 34

1. The right to set up foundations for purposes of general interest is recognized in accordance with the law.
2. The provisions of subsections 2 and 4 of section 22 shall also be applicable to foundations.

Section 35

1. All Spaniards have the duty to work and the right to work, to the free choice of profession or trade, to advancement through work, and to a sufficient remuneration for the satisfaction of their needs and those of their families. Under no circumstances may they be discriminated on account of their sex.
2. The law shall regulate a Workers' Statute.

Section 36

The law shall regulate the pecularities of the legal status of Professional Associations and the exercise of degree professions. The internal structure and the functioning of Associations must be democratic.

Section 37

1. The law shall guarantee the right to collective labour bargaining between workers and employers' representatives, as well as the binding force of the agreements.
2. The right of workers and employers to adopt collective labour dispute measures is hereby recognized. The law regulating the exercise of this right

shall, without prejudice to the restrictions which it may impose, include the guarantees necessary to ensure the functioning of essential public services.

Section 38

Free enterprise is recognized within the framework of a market economy. The public authorities guarantee and protect its exercise and the safeguarding of productivity in accordance with the demands of the general economy and, as the case may be, of economic planning.

CHAPTER 3

Principles governing Economic and Social Policy

Section 39

1. The public authorities ensure social, economic and legal protection of the family.
2. The public authorities likewise ensure full protection of children, who are equal before the law, regardless of their parentage, and of mothers, whatever their marital status. The law shall provide for the possibility of the investigation of paternity.
3. Parents must provide their children, whether born within or outside wedlock, with assistance of every kind while they are still under age and in other circumstances in which the law so establishes.
4. Children shall enjoy the protection provided for in the international agreements safeguarding their rights.

Section 40

1. The public authorities shall promote favourable conditions for social and economic progress and for a more equitable distribution of regional and personal income within the framework of a policy of economic stability. They shall in particular carry out a policy aimed at full employment.
2. Likewise, the public authorities shall promote a policy guaranteeing professional training and retraining; they shall ensure labour safety and hygiene and shall provide for the need of rest by limiting the duration of working day, by periodic paid holidays, and by promoting suitable centres.

Section 41

The public authorities shall maintain a public Social Security system for all citizens guaranteeing adequate social assistance and benefits in situations of hardship, especially in case of unemployment. Supplementary assistance and benefits shall be optional.

Section 42

The State shall be especially concerned with safeguarding the economic and social rights of Spanish workers abroad, and shall direct its policy towards their return.

Section 43

1. The right to health protection is recognized.
2. It is incumbent upon the public authorities to organize and watch over public health by means of preventive measures and the necessary benefits and services. The law shall establish the rights and duties of all in this respect.
3. The public authorities shall foster health education, physical education and sports.
Likewise, they shall encourage the proper use of leisure time.

Section 44

1. The public authorities shall promote and watch over access to culture, to which all are entitled.
2. The public authorities shall promote science and scientific and technical research for the benefit of the general interest.

Section 45

1. Everyone has the right to enjoy an environment suitable for the development of the person, as well as the duty to preserve it.
2. The public authorities shall watch over a rational use of all natural resources with a view to protecting and improving the quality of life and preserving and restoring the environment, by relying on an indispensable collective solidarity.
3. For those who break the provisions contained in the foregoing paragraph, criminal or, where applicable, administrative sanctions shall be imposed, under the terms established by the law, and they shall be obliged to repair the damage caused.

Section 46

The public authorities shall guarantee the preservation and promote the enrichment of the historical, cultural and artistic heritage of the peoples of Spain and of the property of which it consists, regardless of their legal status and their ownership. The criminal law shall punish any offences against this heritage.

Section 47

All Spaniards have the right to enjoy decent and adequate housing. The public authorities shall promote the necessary conditions and establish appropriate standards in order to make this right effective, regulating land use in accordance with the general interest in order to prevent speculation. The community shall have a share in the benefits accruing from the town-planning policies of public bodies.

Section 48

The public authorities shall promote conditions for the free and effective participation of young people in political, social, economic and cultural development.

Section 49

The public authorities shall carry out a policy of preventive care, treatment, rehabilitation and integration of the physically, sensorially and mentally handicapped by giving them the specialized care they require, and affording them special protection for the enjoyment of the rights granted by this Part to all citizens.

Section 50

The public authorities shall guarantee, through adequate and periodically updated pensions, a sufficient income for citizens in old age. Likewise, and without prejudice to the obligations of the families, they shall promote their welfare through a system of social services that provides for their specific problems of health, housing, culture and leisure.

Section 51

1. The public authorities shall guarantee the protection of consumers and users and shall, by means of effective measures, safeguard their safety, health and legitimate economic interests.
2. The public authorities shall promote the information and education of consumers and users, foster their organizations, and hear them on those matters affecting their members, under the terms established by law.
3. Within the framework of the provisions of the foregoing paragraphs, the law shall regulate domestic trade and the system of licensing commercial products.

Section 52

The law shall regulate the professional organizations which contribute to the defence of their own economic interests. Their internal structure and their functioning must be democratic.

CHAPTER 4

Guarantee of Fundamental Rights and Freedoms

Section 53

1. The rights and freedoms recognized in Chapter 2 of the present Part are binding on all public authorities. Only by an act which in any case must respect their essential content, could the exercise of such rights and freedoms be regulated, which shall be protected in accordance with the provisions of section 161(1) a).
2. Any citizen may assert a claim to protect the freedoms and rights recognized in section 14 and in division 1 of Chapter 2, by means of a preferential and summary procedure before the ordinary courts and, when appropriate, by lodging an individual appeal for protection (recurso de amparo) to the Constitutional Court. This latter procedure shall be applicable to conscientious objection as recognized in section 30.
3. Recognition, respect and protection of the principles recognized in Chapter 3 shall guide legislation, judicial practice and actions by the public authorities. They may only be invoked before the ordinary courts in accordance with the legal provisions implementing them.

Section 54

An organic act shall regulate the institution of the Defender of the People (Defensor del Pueblo) as high commissioner of the Cortes Generales, appointed by them to defend the rights contained in this Part; for this purpose he or she may supervise the activity of the Administration and report thereon to the Cortes Generales. (Senate Standing Orders, section 183).

CHAPTER 5

Suspension of Rights and Freedoms

Section 55

1. The rights recognized in sections 17 and 18, subsections 2 and 3, sections 19 and 20, subsection 1, paragraphs a) and d), and subsection 5; sections 21 and 28, subsection 2, and section 37, subsection 2, may be suspended when a state of emergency or siege (martial law) is declared under the terms provided in the Constitution. Subsection 3 of section 17 is excepted from the foregoing provisions in the event of the declaration of a state of emergency.
2. An organic act may determine the manner and the circumstances in which, on an individual basis and with the necessary participation of the courts and proper parliamentary control, the rights recognized in section 17, subsection 2, and 18, subsections 2 and 3, may be suspended for specific persons in connection with investigations of the activities of armed bands or terrorist groups.
Unwarranted or abusive use of the powers recognized in the foregoing organic act shall give rise to criminal liability as a violation of the rights and freedoms recognized by the laws.

PART II

The Crown

Section 56

1 The King is the Head of State, the symbol of its unity and permanence. He arbitrates and moderates the regular functioning of the institutions, assumes the highest representationof the Spanish State in international relations, especially with the nations of its historical community, and exercises the functions expressly conferred on him by the Constitution and the laws.
2. His title is that of King of Spain, and he may use the other titles appertaining to the Crown.
3. The person of the King is inviolable and shall not be held accountable. His acts shall always be countersigned in the manner established in section 64. Without such countersignature they shall not be valid, except as provided under section 65(2).

Section 57

1. The Crown of Spain shall be inherited by the successors of H. M. Juan Carlos I de Borbón, the legitimate heir of the historic dynasty. Succession to the throne shall follow the regular order of primogeniture and representation, the first line always having preference over subsequent lines; within the same line, the closer

grade over the more remote; within the same grade, the male over the female, and in the same sex, the elder over the younger.

2. The Crown Prince, from his birth or from the time he acquires the claim, shall hold the title of Prince of Asturias and the other titles traditionally held by the heir to the Crown of Spain.

3. Should all the lines designated by law become extinct, the Cortes Generales shall provide for succession to the Crown in the manner most suitable to the interests of Spain.

4. Those persons with a right of succession to the throne who marry against the express prohibition of the King and the Cortes Generales, shall be excluded from succession to the Crown, as shall their descendants.

5. Abdications and renunciations and any doubt in fact or in law that may arise in connection with the succession to the Crown shall be settled by an organic act.

Section 58

The Queen consort, or the consort of the Queen, may not assume any constitutional functions, except in accordance with the provisions for the Regency.

Section 59

1. In the event of the King being under age, the King's father or mother or, in default thereof, the oldest relative of legal age who is nearest in succession to the Crown, according to the order established in the Constitution, shall immediately assume the office of Regent, which shall exercise during the King's minority.

2. If the King becomes unfit for the exercise of his authority, and this incapacity is recognized by the Cortes Generales, the Crown Prince shall immediately assume the Regency, if he is of age. If he is not, the procedure outlined in the foregoing paragraph shall apply until the coming of age of the Crown Prince.

3. If there is no person entitled to assume the Regency, it shall be appointed by the Cortes Generales and shall be composed of one, three or five persons.

4. In order to exercise the Regency, it is necessary to be Spaniard and legally of age.

5. The Regency shall be exercised by constitutional mandate, and always on behalf of the King.

Section 60

1. The guardian of the King during his minority shall be the person appointed in the will of the deceased King, provided that he or she is of age and Spaniard by birth. If a guardian has not been appointed, the father or the mother shall be guardian, as long as they remain widowed. In default thereof, the guardian shall be appointed by the Cortes Generales, but the offices of Regent and Guardian

may not be held by the same person, except by the father, mother or direct ancestors of the King.
2. Exercise of the guardianship is also incompatible with the holding of any office or political representation.

Section 61

1. The King, on being proclaimed before the Cortes Generales, will swear to faithfully carry out his duties, to obey the Constitution and the laws and ensure that they are obeyed, and to respect the rights of citizens and the Self-governing Communities.
2. The Crown Prince, on coming of age, and the Regent or Regents, on assuming office, will swear the same oath as well as that of loyalty to the King.

Section 62

It is incumbent upon the King:
a) To sanction and promulgate the laws.
b) To summon and dissolve the Cortes Generales and to call for elections under the terms provided for in the Constitution.
c) To call for a referendum in the cases provided for in the Constitution.
d) To propose a candidate for President of the Government and, as the case may be, appoint him or her or remove him or her from office, as provided in the Constitution.
e) To appoint and dismiss members of the Government on the President of the Government's proposal.
f) To issue the decrees approved in the Council of Ministers, to confer civil and military positions and award honours and distinctions in conformity with the law.
g) To be informed of the affairs of State and, for this purpose, to preside over the meetings of the Council of Ministers whenever, he sees fit, at the President of the Government's request.
h) To exercise supreme command of the Armed Forces.
i) To exercise the right of clemency in accordance with the law, which may not authorize general pardons.
j) To exercise the High Patronage of the Royal Academies.

Section 63

1. The King accredits ambassadors and other diplomatic representatives. Foreign representatives in Spain are accredited before him.
2. It is incumbent upon the King to express the State's assent to international commitments through treaties, in conformity with the Constitution and the laws.
3. It is incumbent upon the King, following authorization by the Cortes Generales, to declare war and to make peace.

Section 64

1. The King's acts shall be countersigned by the President of the Government and, when appropriate, by the competent ministers. The nomination and appointment of the President of the Government and the dissolution provided for under section 99, shall be
countersigned by the Speaker of the Congress.
2. The persons countersigning the King's acts shall be liable for them.

Section 65

1. The King receives an overall amount from the State Budget for the maintenance of his Family and Household and distributes it freely.
2. The King freely appoints and dismisses civil and military members of his Household.

PART III

The Cortes Generales

CHAPTER 1

Houses of Parliament

Section 66

1. The Cortes Generales represent the Spanish people and shall consist of the Congress and the Senate.
2. The Cortes Generales exercise the legislative power of the State and adopt its Budget, control the action of the Government and have the other competences assigned by the Constitution.
3. The Cortes Generales are inviolable.

Section 67

1. No one may be a member of both Houses simultaneously, or be a representative in the Assembly of a Self-governing Community and a Member of Congress at the same time.
2. Members of the Cortes Generales shall not be bound by any compulsory mandate.
3. Meetings of members of Parliament which are held without having been called in the statutory manner, shall not be binding on the Houses, and members may not exercise their functions nor enjoy their privileges.

Section 68

1. The Congress shall consist of a minimum of three hundred and a maximum of four hundred Members, elected by universal, free, equal, direct and secret suffrage, under the terms to be laid down by the law.
2. The electoral constituency is the province. The cities of Ceuta and Melilla shall be represented by one Member each. The total number of Members shall be distributed in accordance with the law, each constituency being allotted a minimum initial representation and the remainder being distributed in proportion to the population.
3. The election in each constituency shall be conducted on the basis of proportional representation.
4. The Congress is elected for four years. The term of office of Members thereof ends four years after their election or on the day on which the Congress is dissolved.
5. All Spaniards entitled to the full exercise of their political rights shall be electors and may be elected.
The law shall recognize and the State shall facilitate the exercise of the right of vote by Spaniards who are outside Spanish territory.
6. Elections shall take place between thirty and sixty days after the end of the previous term of office. The Congress so elected must be convened within twenty-five days following the holding of elections.

Section 69

1. The Senate is the House of territorial representation.
2. In each province, four Senators shall be elected by the voters thereof by universal, free, equal, direct and secret suffrage, under the terms to be laid down by an organic act.
3. In the insular provinces, each island or group of islands with a Cabildo or insular Council shall be a constituency for the purpose of electing Senators; there shall be three Senators for each of the major islands --Gran Canaria, Mallorca and Tenerife-- and one for each of the following islands or groups of islands: Ibiza-Formentera, Menorca, Fuerteventura, Gomera, Hierro, Lanzarote and La Palma.
4. The cities of Ceuta and Melilla shall elect two Senators each.
5. The Self-governing Communities shall, in addition, appoint one Senator and a further Senator for every million inhabitants in their respective territories. The appointment shall be incumbent upon the Legislative Assembly or, in default thereof, upon the Selfgoverning Community's highest corporate body as provided for by its Statute which shall, in any case, guarantee adequate proportional representation.
6. The Senate is elected for four years. The Senators' term of office shall end four years after their election or on the day on which the House is dissolved.

Section 70

1. The Electoral Act shall establish grounds for ineligibility and incompatibility for Members of Congress and Senators, which shall in any case include those who are:
a) Members of the Constitutional Court.
b) High officers of the State Administration as laid down by law, with the exception of the members of the Government.
c) The Defender of the People.
d) Magistrates, Judges and Public Prosecutors when in office.
e) Professional soldiers and members of the Security and Police Forces and Corps in active service.
f) Members of the Electoral Commissions.
2. The validity of the certificates of election and credentials of members of each House shall be subject to judicial control, under the terms to be laid down in the Electoral Act.

Section 71

1. Members of Congress and Senators shall enjoy freedom of speech for opinions expressed in the exercise of their functions.
2. During their term of office, Members of Congress and Senators shall likewise enjoy freedom from arrest and may be arrested only in the event of flagrante delicto. They may be neither indicted nor tried without prior authorization of their respective House.
3. In criminal proceedings brought against Members of Congress and Senators, the competent court shall be the Criminal Section of the Supreme Court.
4. Members of Congress and Senators shall receive a salary to be determined by the respective House.

Section 72

1. The Houses lay down their own Standing Orders, adopt their budgets autonomously and, by common agreement, regulate the Personnel Statute of the Cortes Generales. The Standing Orders and their reform shall be subject to a final vote over the whole text, which shall require the overall majority.
2. The Houses elect their respective Speakers and the other members of their Bureaus. Joint sittings shall be presided over by the Speaker of the Congress and shall be governed by the Standing Orders of the Cortes Generales approved by the overall majority of members of each House.
3. The Speakers of the Houses shall exercise on their behalf all administrative powers and disciplinary functions within its premises.

Section 73

1 The Houses shall meet annually for two ordinary periods of sessions: the first from September to December, and the second from February to June.
2. The Houses may meet in extraordinary sessions at the request of the Government, of the Permanent Deputation or of the overall majority of members of either of the two Houses. Extraordinary sessions must be convened with a specific agenda and shall be adjourned once this has been dealt with.

Section 74

1. The Houses shall meet in joint session in order to exercise the non-legislative powers expressly conferred upon the Cortes Generales by Part II.
2. The decisions of the Cortes Generales specified in sections 94(1), 145(2) and 158(2) shall be taken by a majority vote of each of the Houses. In the first case, the procedure shall be initiated by the Congress, and in the remaining two by the Senate. In any case, if an agreement is not reached between the Senate and the Congress, an attempt to reach agreement shall be made by a Mixed Committee consisting of an equal number of Members of Congress and Senators. The Committee shall submit a text which shall be voted on by both Houses. If this is not approved in the established manner, the Congress shall decide by overall majority.

Section 75

1. The Houses shall convene in Plenary sittings and in Committees.
2. The Houses may delegate to Standing Legislative Committees the approval of Government or non-governmental bills. However, the Plenary sitting may at any time demand that any Government or non-governmental bill that has been so delegated be debated and voted upon by the Plenary itself.
3. Excluded from the provisions of the foregoing paragraph are constitutional reform, international affairs, organic and basic acts and the Budget.

Section 76

1. The Congress and the Senate and, when appropriate, both Houses jointly, may appoint enquiry committees on any matter of public interest. Their conclusions shall not be binding on the Courts, nor shall they affect judicial decisions, but the results of investigations may be referred to the Public Prosecutor for the exercise of appropriate action whenever necessary.
2. It shall be compulsory to appear when summoned by the Houses. The law shall regulate penalties to be imposed for failure to comply with this obligation.

Section 77

1. The Houses may receive individual and collective petitions, always in writing; direct submission by citizens' demonstrations is prohibited.
2. The Houses may refer such petitions to the Government. The Government shall provide an explanation regarding their content, when required to do so by the Houses.

Section 78

1. In each House there shall be a Permanent Deputation (Diputación Permanente) consisting of a minimum of twenty-one members who shall represent the parliamentary groups in proportion to their numerical importance.
2. The Permanent Deputation shall be presided over by the Speaker of the respective House and their functions shall be that provided in section 73, that of assuming the powers of the Houses in accordance with sections 86 and 116 in case that the latter have been dissolved or their terms have expired, and that of safeguarding the powers of the Houses when they are not in session.
3. On the expiration of the term or in case of dissolution, the Permanent Deputations shall continue to exercise their functions until the constitution of the new Cortes Generales.
4. When the House concerned meets, the Permanent Deputation shall report on the matters dealt with and on its decisions.

Section 79

1. In order to adopt agreements, the Houses must meet in statutory manner, with the majority of their members present.
2. In order to be valid, such agreements must be approved by the majority of the members present, without prejudice to the special majorities that may be required by the Constitution or the organic acts and those which are provided for by the Standing Orders of the Houses for the election of persons.
3. The vote of Senators and Members of Congress shall be personal and may not be delegated.

Section 80

Plenary meetings of the Houses shall be public, except when otherwise decided by each House by overall majority, or in accordance with the Standing Orders.

CHAPTER 2

Drafting of Bills

Section 81

1. Organic acts are those relating to the implementation of fundamental rights and public freedoms, those approving the Statutes of Autonomy and the general electoral system and other laws provided for in the Constitution.
2. The approval, amendment or repeal of organic acts shall require the overall majority of the Members of Congress in a final vote on the bill as a whole.

Section 82

1. The Cortes Generales may delegate to the Government the power to issue rules with the force of an act of the Parliament on specific matters not included in the foregoing section.
2. Legislative delegation must be granted by means of act of basic principles when its purpose is to draw up texts in sections, or by an ordinary act when it is a matter of consolidating several legal statutes into one.
3. Legislative delegation must be expressly granted to the Government for a concrete matter and with a fixed time limit for its exercise. The delegation shall expire when the Government has made use of it through the publication of the corresponding regulation. It may not be construed as having been granted implicitly or for an indeterminate period. Nor shall sub-delegation to authorities other than the Government itself be authorized.
4. Acts of basic principles shall define precisely the purpose and scope of legislative delegation, as well as the principles and criteria to be followed in its exercise.
5. Authorization for consolidating legal texts shall determine the legislative scope implicit in the delegation, specifying if it is restricted to the mere drafting of a single text or whether it includes regulating, clarifying and harmonizing the legal statutes to be consolidated.
6. The acts of delegation may provide for additional control devices in each case, without prejudice to the jurisdiction of the Courts.

Section 83

The acts of basic principles may in no case:
a) Authorize the modification of the act itself.
b) Grant power to enact retroactive regulations.

Section 84

In the event that a non-governmental bill or an amendment is contrary to a currently valid legislative delegation, the Government may oppose its processing.

In this case, a nongovernmental bill may be submitted for the total or partial repeal of the delegation act.

Section 85

Government provisions containing delegated legislation shall bear the title of "Legislative Decrees".

Section 86

1. In case of extraordinary and urgent need, the Government may issue temporary legislative provisions which shall take the form of decree-laws and which may not affect the legal system of the basic State institutions, the rights, duties and freedoms of the citizens contained in Part 1, the system of Self-governing Communities, or the general electoral law.
2. Decree-laws must be inmediately submitted for debate and voting by the entire Congress, which must be summoned for this purpose if not already in session, within thirty days of their promulgation. The Congress shall adopt an specific decision on their ratification or repeal in the said period, for which purpose the Standing Orders shall contemplate a special summary procedure.
3. During the period referred to in the foregoing subsection, the Cortes may process them as Government bills by means of the urgency procedure.

Section 87

1. Legislative initiative belongs to the Government, the Congress and the Senate, in accordance with the Constitution and the Standing Orders of the Houses.
2. The Assemblies of Self-governing Communities may request the Government to adopt a bill or may refer a non-governmental bill to the Bureau of Congress and delegate a maximum of three Assembly members to defend it.
3. An organic act shall lay down the manner and the requirements of the popular initiative for submission of non-governmental bills. In any case, no less than 500.000 authenticated signatures shall be required. This initiative shall not be allowed on matters concerning organic acts, taxation, international affairs or the prerogative of pardon.

Section 88

Government bills shall be approved by the Council of Ministers which shall refer them to the Congress, attaching a statement setting forth the necessary grounds and facts to reach a decision thereon.

Section 89

1. The reading of non-governmental bills shall be regulated by the Standing Orders of the Houses in such a way that the priority attached to Government bills

shall not prevent the exercise of the right to propose legislation under the terms laid down in section 87.
2. Non-governmental bills which, in accordance with section 87, are taken under consideration in the Senate, shall be referred to the Congress for reading.

Section 90

1. An organic act shall lay down the terms and procedures for the different kinds of referendum provided for in this Constitution.
2. Within two months after receiving the text, the Senate may, by a message stating the reasons for it, adopt a veto or approve amendments thereto. The veto must be adopted by overall majority. The bill may not be submitted to the King for assent unless, in the event of veto, the Congress has ratified the initial text by overall majority or by single majority if two months have elapsed since its introduction, or has reached a decision as to the amendments, accepting them or not by single majority.
3. The period of two months allowed to the Senate for vetoing or amending a bill shall be reduced to twenty calendar days for bills declared by the Government or by the Congress to be urgent.

Section 91

The King shall, within a period of fifteen days, give his assent to bills drafted by the Cortes Generales, and shall promulgate them and order their publication forthwith.

Section 92

1. Political decisions of special importance may be submitted to all citizens in a consultative referendum.
2. The referendum shall be called by the King on the President of the Government's proposal after previous authorization by the Congress.
3. An organic act shall lay down the terms and procedures for the different kinds of referendum provided for in this Constitution.

CHAPTER 3

International Treaties

Section 93

Authorization may be granted by an organic act for concluding treaties by which powers derived from the Constitution shall be transferred to an international organization or institution. It is incumbent on the Cortes Generales or the Government, as the case may be, to ensure compliance with these treaties and with resolutions originating in the international and supranational organizations to which such powers have been sotransferred.

Section 94

1. The giving of the consent of the State to enter any commitment by means of treaty or agreement, shall require prior authorization of the Cortes Generales in the following cases:
a) Treaties of a political nature.
b) Treaties or agreements of a military nature.
c) Treaties or agreements affecting the territorial integrity of the State or the fundamental rights and duties established under Part 1.
d) Treaties or agreements which imply financial liabilities for the Public Treasury.
e) Treaties or agreements which involve amendment or repeal of some law or require legislative measures for their execution.
2) The Congress and the Senate shall be informed forthwith of the conclusion of any other treaties or agreements.

Section 95

1. The conclusion of an international treaty containing stipulations contrary to the Constitution shall require prior constitutional amendment.
2) The Government or either House may request the Constitutional Court to declare whether or not such a contradiction exists.

Section 96

1. Validly concluded international treaties, once officially published in Spain, shall be part of the internal legal system. Their provisions may only be repealed, amended or suspended in the manner provided for in the treaties themselves or in accordance with the general rules of international law.
2. The procedure provided for in section 94 for entering into international treaties and agreements shall be used for denouncing them.

PART IV

Government and Administration

Section 97

The Government shall conduct domestic and foreign policy, civil and military administration and the defence of the State. It exercises executive authority and the power of statutory regulations in accordance with the Constitution and the laws.

Section 98

1. The Government shall consist of the President, Vice-Presidents, when appropiate, Ministers and other members as may be created by law.
2. The President shall direct the Governments' action and coordinate the functions of the other members thereof, without prejudice to the competence and direct responsability of the latter in the discharge of their duties.
3. Members of the Government may not perform representative functions other than those derived from their parliamentary mandate, nor any other public function not deriving from their office, nor engage in any professional or commercial activity whatsoever.
4. The status and incompatibilities of members of the Government shall be laid down by law.

Section 99

1. After each renewal of the Congress and in the other cases provided for under the Constitution, the King shall, after consultation with the representatives appointed by the political groups with parliamentary representation, and through the Speaker of the Congress, nominate a candidate for the Presidency of the Government.
2. The candidate nominated in accordance with the provisions of the foregoing subsection shall submit to the Congress the political programme of the Government he or she intends to form and shall seek the confidence of the House.
3. If the Congress, by vote of the overall majority of its members, grants to said candidate its confidence, the King shall appoint him or her President. If overall majority is not obtained, the same proposal shall be submitted for a fresh vote forty-eight hours after the previous vote, and confidence shall be deemed to have been secured if granted by single majority.
4. If, after this vote, confidence for the investiture has not been obtained, successive proposals shall be voted upon in the manner provided for in the foregoing paragraphs.
5. If within two months of the first vote for investiture no candidate has obtained the confidence of the Congress, the King shall dissolve both Houses and call for new elections, with the countersignature of the Speaker of the Congress.

Section 100

The other members of the Government shall be appointed and dismissed by the King at the President's proposal.

Section 101

1. The Government shall resign after the holding of general elections, in the event of loss of parliamentary confidence as provided in the Constitution, or on the resignation or death of the President.
2. The outgoing Government shall continue as acting body until the new Government takes office.

Section 102

1. The President and other members of the Government shall be held criminally liable, should the occasion arise, before the Criminal Section of the Supreme Court.
2. If the charge were treason or any offence against the security of the State committed in the discharge of office, it may only be brought against them on the initiative of one quarter of Members of Congress and with the approval of the overall majority thereof.
3. The Royal prerogative of pardon shall not apply any of the cases provided for under the present section.

Section 103

1. The Public Administration shall serve the general interest in a spirit of objectivity and shall act in accordance with the principles of efficiency, hierarchy, decentralization, deconcentration and coordination, and in full subordination to the law.
2. The organs of State Administration are set up, directed and coordinated in accordance with the law.
3. The law shall lay down the status of civil servants, the entry into the civil service in accordance with the principles of merit and ability, the special features of the exercise of their right to union membership, the system of incompatibilities and the guarantees regarding impartiality in the discharge of their duties.

Section 104

1. The Security Forces and Corps serving under the Government shall have the duty to protect the free exercise of rights and freedoms and to guarantee the safety of citizens.
2. An organic act shall specify the duties, basic principles of action and statutes of the Security Forces and Corps.

Section 105

The law shall make provision for:

a) The hearing of citizens, directly, or through the organizations and associations recognized by the law, in the process of drawing up the administrative provisions which affect them.
b) The access of citizens to administrative files and records, except to the extent that they may concern the security and defence of the State, the investigation of crimes and the privacy of persons.
c) The procedures for the taking of administrative action, with due safeguards for the hearing of interested parties when appropriate.

Section 106

1. The Courts shall check the power to issue regulations and ensure that the rule of law prevails in administrative action, and that the latter is subordinated to the ends which justify it.
2. Private individuals shall, under the terms laid down by law, be entitled to compensation for any harm they may suffer in any of their property and rights, except in cases of force majeure, whenever such harm is the result of the operation of public services.

Section 107

The Council of State is the supreme consultative body of the Government. An organic act shall make provision for its membership and its terms of reference.

PART V

Relations between the Government and the Cortes Generales

Section 108

The Government is jointly accountable before the Congress for its conduct of political business.

Section 109

The Houses and their Committees may, through their respective Speaker, request any kind of information and help they may need from the Government and Government Departments and from any authorities of the State and Selfgoverning Communities.

Section 110

1. The Houses and their Committees may summon members of the Government.

2. Members of the Government are entitled to attend meetings of the Houses and their Committees and to be heard in them and may request that officials from their Departments are allowed to report to them.

Section 111

1. The Government and each of its members are subject to interpellations and questions put to them in the Houses. The Standing Orders shall set aside a minimum weekly time for this type of debate.
2. Any interpellation may give rise to a motion in which the House states its position.

Section 112

The President of the Government, after deliberation by the Council of Ministers, may ask the Congress for a vote of confidence in favour of his or her programme or of a general policy statement. Confidence shall be deemed to have been obtained when a single majority of the Members of Congress vote in favour.

Section 113

1. The Congress may require political responsibility from the Government by adopting a motion of censure by overall majority of its Members.
2. The motion of censure must be proposed by at least one tenth of the Members of Congress and shall include a candidate for the office of the Presidency of the Government.
3. The motion of censure may not be voted until five days after it has been submitted.During the first two days of this period, alternative motions may be submitted.
4. If the motion of censure is not adopted by the Congress, its signatories may not submit another during the same period of sessions.

Section 114

1. If the Congress withholds its confidence from the Government, the latter shall submit its resignation to the King, whereafter the President of the Government shall be nominated in accordance with the provisions of section 99.
2. If the Congress adopts a motion of censure, the Government shall submit its resignation to the King, and the candidate proposed in the motion of censure shall be deemed to have the confidence of the House for the purposes provided in section 99. The King shall appoint him or her President of the Government.

Section 115

1. The President of the Government, after deliberation by the Council of Ministers, and under his or her sole responsibility, may propose the dissolution of

the Congress, the Senate or the Cortes Generales, which shall be proclaimed by the King. The decree of dissolution shall set a date for the elections.
2. The proposal for dissolution may not be submitted while a motion of censure is pending.
3. There shall be no further dissolution until a year has elapsed since the previous one, except as provided for in section 99, subsection 5.

Section 116

1. An organic act shall make provision for the states of alarm, emergency and siege (martial law) and the powers and restrictions attached to each of them.
2. A state of alarm shall be proclaimed by the Government, by means of a decree agreed in Council of Ministers, for a maximum period of fifteen days. The Congress shall be informed and must meet immediately, and without its authorization the said period may not be extended. The decree shall specify the territory to which the effects of the proclamation apply.
3. A state of emergency shall be proclaimed by the Government by decree agreed in Council of Ministers, after prior authorization by the Congress. The authorization for and proclamation of a state of emergency must specifically state the effects thereof, the territory to which it is to apply and its duration, which may not exceed thirty days, subject to extension for a further thirty-day period, with the same requirements.
4. A state of siege (martial law) shall be proclaimed by overall majority of Congress solely on the Government's proposal. Congress shall determine its territorial extension, duration and terms.
5. The Congress may not be dissolved while any of the states referred to in the present section remains in force, and if the Houses are not in session, they shall be automatically convened. Their functioning, as well as that of the other constitutional State authorities, may not be interrupted while any of these states is in force.
If, in the event that the Congress has been dissolved or its term has expired, a situation giving rise to any of these states should occur, the powers of the Congress shall be assumed by its Permanent Deputation.
6. Proclamation of states of alarm, emergency and siege shall not affect the principle of liability of the Government or its agents as recognized in the Constitution and the laws.

PART VI

Judicial Power

Section 117

1. Justice emanates from the people and is administered on behalf of the King by judges and magistrates members of the Judicial Power who shall be

independent, shall have fixity of tenure, shall be accountable for their acts and subject only to the rule of law.

2. Judges and magistrates may only be dismissed, suspended, transferred or retired on the grounds and subject to the safeguards provided for by the law.

3. The exercise of judicial authority in any kind of action, both in ruling and having judgments executed, is vested exclusively in the courts and tribunals laid down by the law, in accordance with the rules of jurisdiction and procedure which may be established therein.

4. Judges and courts shall not exercise any powers other than those indicated in the foregoing subsection and those which are expressly allocated to them by law as a guarantee of any right.

5. The principle of jurisdictional unity is the basis of the organization and operation of the courts. The law shall make provision for the exercise of military jurisdiction strictly within military framework and in cases of state of siege (martial law), in accordance with the principles of the Constitution.

6. Courts of exception are prohibited.

Section 118

It is compulsory to comply with sentences and other final resolutions of judges and courts, as well as to pay them such assistance as they may require in the course of trials and for the execution of judgments.

Section 119

Justice shall be free when thus provided for by law, and shall in any case be so in respect of those who have insufficient means to sue in court.

Section 120

1. Judicial proceedings shall be public, with the exceptions contemplated in the laws on procedure.

2. Proceedings shall be predominantly oral, especially in criminal cases.

3. Judgments shall always specify the grounds therefore, and they shall be delivered in a public hearing.

Section 121

Damages caused by judicial error as well as those arising from irregularities in the administration of justice shall give rise to a right to compensation by the State, in accordance with the law.

Section 122

1. The Organic Act of the Judicial Power shall make provision for the setting up, operation and internal administration of courts and tribunals as well as for the legal status of professional judges and magistrates, who shall form a single body, and of the staff serving in the administration of justice.
2. The General Council of the Judicial Power is its governing body. An organic act shall lay down its status and the system of incompatibilities applicable to its members and their functions, especially in connection with appointments, promotions, inspection and the disciplinary system.
3. The General Council of the Judicial Power shall consist of the President of the Supreme Court, who shall preside it, and of twenty members appointed by the King for a five-year period, of which twelve shall be judges and magistrates of all judicial categories, under the terms provided for by the organic act; four nominated by the Congress and four by the Senate, elected in both cases by three-fifths of their members amongst lawyers and other jurists of acknowledged competence with more than fifteen years of professional practice.

Section 123

1. The Supreme Court, with jurisdiction over the whole of Spain, is the highest judicial body in all branches of justice, except with regard to provisions concerning constitutional guarantees.
2. The President of the Supreme Court shall be appointed by the King, on the General Council of the Judicial Power proposal in the manner to be laid down by the law.

Section 124

1 The Office of Public Prosecutor, without prejudice to functions entrusted to other bodies, has the task of promoting the operation of justice in the defence of the rule of law, of citizens' rights and of the public interest as safeguarded by the law, whether ex officio or at the request of interested parties, as well as that of protecting the independence of the courts and securing before them the satisfaction of social interest.
2. The Office of Public Prosecutor shall discharge its duties through its own bodies in accordance with the principles of unity of operation and hierarchical subordination, subject in all cases to the principles of the rule of law and of impartiality.
3. The organic statute of the Office of the Public Prosecutor shall be laid down by law.
4. The State's Public Prosecutor shall be appointed by the King on the Government's proposal after consultation with the General Council of the Judicial Power.

Section 125

Citizens may engage in popular action and take part in the administration of justice through the institution of the jury, in the manner and with respect to those criminal trials as may be determined by law, as well as in customary and traditional courts.

Section 126

The judicial police shall report to the judges, the courts and the Public Prosecutor when discharging their duties of crime investigation and the discovery and arrest of offenders, under the terms to be laid down by the law.

Section 127

1. Judges and magistrates as well as public prosecutors, whilst actively in office, may not hold other public office nor belong to political parties or unions. The law shall make provision for the system and methods of professional association for judges, magistrates and prosecutors.
2. The law shall make provision for the system of incompatibilities for members of the Judicial Power, which must ensure their total independence.

PART VII

Economy and Finance

Section 128

1. The entire wealth of the country in its different forms, irrespective of ownership, shall be subordinated to the general interest.
2. Public initiative in economic activity is recognized. Essential resources or services may be reserved by law to the public sector especially in the case of monopolies. Likewise, State intervention in companies may be imposed when the public interest so demands.

Section 129

1. The law shall establish the forms of participation of the persons concerned in Social Security and in the activities of those public bodies whose operation directly affects quality of life or general welfare.
2. The public authorities shall efficiently promote the various forms of participation in the enterprise and shall encourage cooperative societies by means of appropriate legislation.

They shall also establish means to facilitate access by workers to ownership of the means of production.

Section 130

1. The public authorities shall promote the modernization and development of all economic sectors and, in particular, of agriculture, livestock raising, fishing and handicrafts, in order to bring the standard of living of all Spaniards up to the same level.
2. For the same purpose, special treatment shall be given to mountain areas.

Section 131

1. The State shall be empowered to plan general economic activity by an act in order to meet collective needs, to balance and harmonize regional and sectorial development and to stimulate the growth of income and wealth and their more equitable distribution.
2. The Government shall draft planning projects in accordance with forecasts supplied by Self-governing Communities and with the advice and cooperation of unions and other professional, employers' and financial organizations. A council shall be set up for this purpose, whose membership and duties shall be laid down by the law.

Section 132

1. The law shall lay down the rules governing public and communal property, on the basis that it shall be inalienable, exempt from prescription and cannot be attached under any circumstances, and it shall also provide for the case of disaffectation from public purpose.
2. The goods of the State's public property shall be that established by law and shall, in any case, include the foreshore beaches, territorial waters and the natural resources of the exclusive economic zone and the continental shelf.
3. The State's Domain and the National Heritage, as well as their administration, protection and preservation, shall be regulated by law.

Section 133

1. The primary power to raise taxes is vested exclusively in the State by means of law.
2. Self-governing Communities and local Corporations may impose and levy taxes, in accordance with the Constitution and the laws.
3. Any fiscal benefit affecting State taxes must be established by virtue of law.

4. Public Administrations may only contract financial liabilities and incur expenditures in accordance with the law.

Section 134

1. It is incumbent upon the Government to draft the State Budget and upon the Cortes Generales to examine, amend and adopt it.
2. The State Budget shall be drafted annually and shall include the entire expenditure and income of the State public sector and a specific mention shall be made of the amount of the fiscal benefits affecting State taxes.
3. The Government must submit the draft State Budget to the Congress at least three months before the expiration of that of the previous year.
4. If the Budget Bill is not passed before the first day of the corresponding financial year, the Budget of the previous financial year shall be automatically extended until the new one is approved.
5. Once the Budget Bill has been adopted, the Government may submit bills involving increases in public expenditure or decreases in the revenue corresponding to the same financial year.
6. Any non-governmental bill or amendment which involves an increase in appropriations or a decrease in budget revenue shall require previous approval by the Government before its passage.
7. The Budget Act may not establish new taxes. It may modify them, wherever a tax law of a substantive nature so provides.

Section 135

(This text includes the second constitutional reform adopted on 27/09/2011 ;).

1. All public administrations will conform to the principle of budgetary stability.
2. The State and the Self-governing Communities may not incur a structural deficit that exceeds the limits established by the European Union for their member states.
An Organic Act shall determine the maximum structural deficit the state and the Self-governing Communities may have, in relation to its gross domestic product. Local authorities must submit a balanced budget.
3. The State and the Self-governing Communities must be authorized by Act in order to issue Public Debt bonds or to contract loans.
Loans to meet payment on the interest and capital of the State's Public Debt shall always be deemed to be included in budget expenditure and their payment shall have absolute priority. These appropriations may not be subject to amendment or modification as long as they conform to the terms of issue.
The volume of public debt of all the public administrations in relation to the State' gross domestic product may not exceed the benchmark laid down by the Treaty on the Functioning of the European Union.

4. The limits of the structural deficit and public debt volume may be exceeded only in case of natural disasters, economic recession or extraordinary emergency situations that are beyond the control of the State and significantly impair either the financial situation or the economic or social sustainability of the State, as appreciated by an absolute majority of the members of the Congress of Deputies.
5. An Organic Act shall develop the principles referred to in this article, as well as participation in the respective procedures of the organs of institutional coordination between government fiscal policy and financial support. In any case, the Organic Act shall address:
a) The distribution of the limits of deficit and debt among the different public administrations, the exceptional circumstances to overcome them and the manner and time in which to correct the deviations on each other.
b) The methodology and procedure for calculating the structural deficit.
c) The responsibility of each public administration in case of breach of budgetary stability objectives.
6. The Self-governing Communities, in accordance with their respective laws and within the limits referred to in this article, shall take the appropriate procedures for effective implementation of the principle of stability in their rules and budgetary decisions.

Section 136

1. The Auditing Court is the supreme body charged with auditing the State's accounts and financial management, as well as those of the public sector.
t shall be directly accountable to the Cortes Generales and shall discharge its duties by delegation of the same when examining and verifying the General State Accounts.
2. The State Accounts and those of the State's public sector shall be submitted to the Auditing Court and shall be audited by the latter.
The Auditing Court, without prejudice to its own jurisdiction, shall send an annual report to the Cortes Generales informing them, where applicable, of any infringements that may, in its opinion, have been committed, or any liabilities that may have been incurred.
3. Members of the Auditing Court shall enjoy the same independence and fixity of tenure and shall be subject to the same incompatibilities as judges.
4. An organic act shall make provision for membership, organization and duties of the Auditing Court.

PART VIII

Territorial Organization of the State

CHAPTER 1

General Principles

Section 137

The State is organized territorially into municipalities, provinces and the Selfgoverning Communities that may be constituted. All these bodies shall enjoy selfgovernment for the management of their respective interests.

Section 138

1. The State guarantees the effective implementation of the principle of solidarity proclaimed in section 2 of the Constitution, by endeavouring to establish a fair and adequate economic balance between the different areas of the Spanish territory and taking into special consideration the circumstances pertaining to those which are islands.
2. Differences between Statutes of the different Self-governing Communities may in no case imply economic or social privileges.

Section 139

1. All Spaniards have the same rights and obligations in any part of the State territory.
2. No authority may adopt measures which directly or indirectly hinder freedom of movement and settlement of persons and free movement of goods throughout the Spanish territory.

CHAPTER 2

Local Government

Section 140

The Constitution guarantees the autonomy of municipalities. These shall enjoy full legal personality. Their government and administration shall be vested in their Town Councils, consisting of Mayors and councillors. Councillors shall be elected by residents of the municipality by universal, equal, free, direct and secret suffrage, in the manner provided for by the law. The Mayors shall be elected by the councillors or by the residents. The law shall lay down the terms under which an open council of all residents may proceed.

Section 141

1. The province is a local entity, with its own legal personality, arising from the grouping of municipalities, and a territorial division designed to carry out the activities of the State. Any alteration of provincial boundaries must be approved by the Cortes Generales in an organic act.
2. The government and autonomous administration of the provinces shall be entrusted to Provincial Councils (Diputaciones) or other Corporations that must be representative in character.
3. Groups of municipalities other than provinces may be formed.
4. In the archipelagos, each island shall also have its own administration in the form of Cabildo or Insular Council.

Section 142

Local treasuries must have sufficient funds available in order to perform the tasks assigned by law to the respective Corporations, and shall mainly be financed by their own taxation as well as by their share of State taxes and those of Selfgoverning Communities.

CHAPTER 3

Self-governing Communities

Section 143

1. In the exercise of the right to self-government recognized in section 2 of the Constitution, ordering provinces with common historic, cultural and economic characteristics, insular erritories and provinces with a historic regional status may accede to self-government nd form Self-governing Communities (Comunidades Autónomas) in conformity with he provisions contained in this Part and in the respective Statutes.
2. The right to initiate the process towards self-government lies with all the Provincial ouncils concerned or with the corresponding inter-island body and with two thirds of he municipalities whose population represents at least the majority of the electorate of ach province or island. These requirements must be met within six months from the nitial agreement reached to this aim by any of the local Corporations concerned.

3. If this initiative is not successful, it may be repeated only after five years have elapsed.

Section 144

The Cortes Generales may, in the national interest, and by an organic act:
a) Authorize the setting-up of a Self-governing Community, where its territory does not exceed that of a province and does not possess the characteristics outlined in section 143, paragraph 1.
b) Authorize or grant, as the case may be, a Statute of Autonomy to territories which are not integrated into the provincial organization.
c) Take over the initiative of the local Corporations referred to in section 143, paragraph 2.

Section 145

1. Under no circumstances shall a federation of Self-governing Communities be allowed.
2. Statutes of Autonomy may provide for the circumstances, requirements and terms under which Self-governing Communities may reach agreements among themselves for the management and rendering of services in matters pertaining to them, as well as for the nature and effects of the corresponding notification to be sent to the Cortes Generales. In all other cases, cooperation agreements among Self-governing Communities shall require authorization by the Cortes Generales.

Section 146

The draft Statute of Autonomy shall be drawn up by an assembly consisting of members of the Provincial Council or inter-island body of the provinces concerned, and the respective Members of Congress and Senators elected in them, and shall be sent to the Cortes Generales for its drafting as an Act.

Section 147

1. Within the terms of the present Constitution, Statutes of Autonomy shall be the basic institutional rule of each Self-governing Community and the State shall recognize and protect them as an integral part of its legal system.
2. The Statutes of Autonomy must contain:
a) The name of the Community which best corresponds to its historic identity.
b) Its territorial boundaries.
c) The name, organization and seat of its own autonomous institutions.
d) The powers assumed within the framework laid down by the Constitution and the basic rules for the transfer of the corresponding services.

3. Amendment of Statutes of Autonomy shall conform to the procedure established therein and shall in any case require approval of the Cortes Generales through an organic act.

Section 148

1. The Self-governing Communities may assume competences over the following matters:
1.ª Organization of their institutions of self-government.
2.ª Changes in municipal boundaries within their territory and, in general, functions appertaining to the State Administration regarding local Corporations, whose transfer may be authorized by legislation on local governement.
3.ª Town and country planning and housing.
4.ª Public works of interest to the Self-governing Community, within its own territory.
5.ª Railways and roads whose routes lie exclusively within the territory of the Selfgoverning Community and transport by the above means or by cable fulfilling the same conditions.
6.ª Ports of haven, recreational ports and airports and, in general, those which are not engaged in commercial activities.
7.ª Agriculture and livestock raising, in accordance with general economic planning.
8.ª Woodlands and forestry.
9.ª Management of environmental protection.
10.ª Planning, construction and exploitation of hydraulic projects, canals and irrigation of interest to the Self-governing Community; mineral and thermal waters.
11.ª Inland water fishing, shellfish industry and fishfarming, hunting and river fishing.
12.ª Local fairs.
13.ª Promotion of economic development of the Self-governing Community within the objectives set by national economic policy.
14.ª Handicrafts.
15.ª Museums, libraries and music conservatories of interest to the Self-governing Community.
16.ª The Self-governing Community's monuments of interest.
17.ª The promotion of culture and research and, where applicable, the teaching of the Selfgoverning Community's language.
18.ª The promotion and planning of tourism within its territorial area.
19.ª The promotion of sports and the proper use of leisure.
20.ª Social assistance.
21.ª Health and hygiene.
22.ª The supervision and protection of its buildings and installations. Coordination and other powers relating to local police forces under the terms to be laid down by an organic act.

2. After five years, the Self-governing Communities may, by amendment of their Statutes of Autonomy, progressively enlarge their powers within the framework laid down in section 149.

Section 149

1. The State shall have exclusive competence over the following matters:

1.ª Regulation of basic conditions guaranteeing the equality of all Spaniards in the exercise of their rights and in the fulfilment of their constitutional duties.
2.ª Nationality, immigration, emigration, status of aliens, and right of asylum.
3.ª International relations.
4.ª Defence and the Armed Forces.
5.ª Administration of Justice.
6.ª Commercial, criminal and penitentiary legislation; procedural legislation, without prejudice to the necessary specialities in these fields arising from the peculiar features of the substantive law of the Self-governing Communities.
7.ª Labour legislation, without prejudice to its execution by bodies of the Self-governing Communities.
8.ª Civil legislation, without prejudice to the preservation, modification and development by the Self-governing Communities of their civil law, foral or special, whenever these exist, and traditional charts. In any event rules for the application and effectiveness of legal provisions, civil relations arising from the forms of marriage, keeping of records and drawing up to public instruments, bases of contractual liability, rules for resolving conflicts of law and determination of the sources of law in conformity, in this last case, with the rules of traditional charts or with those of foral or special laws.
9.ª Legislation on copyright and industrial property.
10.ª Customs and tariff regulations; foreign trade.
11.ª Monetary system: foreign currency, exchange and convertibility; bases for the regulations concerning credit, banking and insurance.
12.ª Legislation on weights and measures and determination of the official time.
13.ª Basic rules and coordination of general economic planning.
14.ª General financial affairs and State Debt.
15.ª Promotion and general coordination of scientific and technical research.
16.ª External health measures; basic conditions and general coordination of health matters; legislation on pharmaceutical products.
17.ª Basic legislation and financial system of Social Security, without prejudice to implementation of its services by the Self-governing Communities.
18.ª Basic rules of the legal system of Public Administrations and the status of their officials which shall, in any case, guarantee that all persons under said administrations will receive equal treatment; the common administrative procedure, without prejudice to the special features of the Self-governing Communities' own organizations; legislation on compulsory expropriation; basic legislation on contracts and administrative concessions and the system of liability of all Public Administrations.

19.ª Sea fishing, without prejudice to the powers which, in regulations governing this sector, may be vested to the Self-governing Communities.
20.ª Merchant navy and registering of ships; lighting of coasts and signals at sea; generalinterest ports; general-interest airports; control of the air space, air traffic and transport; meteorological services and aircraft registration.
21.ª Railways and land transport crossing through the territory of more than one Selfgoverning Community; general system of communications; motor vehicle traffic; Post Office services and telecommunications; air and underwater cables and radiocommunications.
22.ª Legislation, regulation and concession of hydraulic resources and development where the water-streams flow through more than one Self-governing Community, and authorization for hydro-electrical power plants whenever their operation affects other Communities or the lines of energy transportation are extended over other Communities.
23.ª Basic legislation on environmental protection, without prejudice to powers of the Self-governing Communities to take additional protective measures; basic legislation on woodlands, forestry and cattle trails.
24.ª Public works of general benefit or whose execution affects more than one Selfgoverning Community.
25.ª Basic regulation of mining and energy.
26.ª Manufacturing, sale, possession and use of arms and explosives
27.ª Basic rules relating to organization of the press, radio and television and, in general, all mass-communications media without prejudice to powers vested in the Self-governing Communities for their development and implementation.
28.ª Protection of Spain's cultural and artistic heritage and national monuments against exportation and spoliation; museums, libraries, and archives belonging to the State, without prejudice to their management by the Self-governing Communities.
29.ª Public safety, without prejudice to the possibility of creation of police forces by the Self-governing Communities, in the manner to be provided for in their respective Statutes of Autonomy and within the framework to be laid down by an organic act.
30.ª Regulation of the requirements for obtention, issue and standardization of academic degrees and professional qualifications and basic rules for implementation of section 27 of the Constitution, in order to guarantee the fulfilment of the duties of public authorities in this matter.
31.ª Statistics for State purposes.
32.ª Authorization of popular consultations through the holding of referendums.
2. Without prejudice to the competences that may be assumed by the Self-governing Communities, the State shall consider the promotion of culture a duty and an essential function and shall facilitate cultural communication among the Self-governing Communities, in cooperation with them.
3. Matters not expressly assigned to the State by this Constitution may fall under the jurisdiction of the Self-governing Communities by virtue of their Statutes of Autonomy. Jurisdiction on matters not claimed by Statutes of Autonomy shall fall

with the State, whose laws shall prevail, in case of conflict, over those of the Self-governing Communities regarding all matters in which exclusive jurisdiction has not been conferred upon the latter. State law shall in any case be suppletory of that of the Self-governing Communities.

Section 150

1. The Cortes Generales, in matters of State jurisdiction, may confer upon all or any of the Self-governing Communities the power to pass legislation for themselves within the framework of the principles, bases and guidelines laid down by a State act. Without prejudice to the jurisdiction of the Courts, each enabling act shall make provision for the method of supervision by the Cortes Generales over the Communities' legislation.
2. The State may transfer or delegate to the Self-governing Communities, through an organic act, some of its powers which by their very nature can be transferred or delegated. The law shall, in each case, provide for the appropriate transfer of financial means, as well as specify the forms of control to be retained by the State.
3. The State may enact laws laying down the necessary principles for harmonizing the rulemaking provisions of the Self-governing Communities, even in the case of matters over which jurisdiction has been vested to the latter, where this is necessary in the general interest. It is incumbent upon the Cortes Generales, by overall majority of the members of each House, to evaluate this necessity.

Section 151

1. It shall not be necessary to wait for the five-year period referred to in section 148, subsection 2, to elapse when the initiative for the autonomy process is agreed upon within the time limit specified in section 143, subsection 2, not only by the corresponding Provincial Councils or inter-island bodies but also by three-quarters of the municipalities of each province concerned, representing at least the majority of the electorate of each one, and said initiative is ratified in a referendum by the overall majority of electors in each province, under the terms to be laid down by an organic act.
2. In the case referred to in the foregoing paragraph, procedure for drafting the Statute of Autonomy shall be as follows:
1.º The Government shall convene all Members of Congress and Senators elected in the constituencies of the territory seeking self-government, in order that they may set themselves up as an Assembly for the sole purpose of drawing up a Statute of Autonomy, to be adopted by the overall majority of its members.
2.º Once the draft Statute has been passed by the Parliamentarians' Assembly, it is to be sent to the Constitutional Committee of the Congress which shall examine it within two months with the cooperation and assistance of a delegation

from the Assembly which has proposed it, in order to decide by common agreement upon its final form.

3.º If such agreement is reached, the resulting text shall be submitted in a referendum to the electorate in the provinces within the territory to be covered by the proposed Statute.

4.º If the draft Statute is approved in each province by the majority of validly cast votes, it shall be referred to the Cortes Generales. Each House, in plenary sitting, shall decide upon the text by means of a vote of ratification. Once the Statute been passed, the King shall give his assent and promulgate it as an act.

5.º If the agreement referred to in paragraph ii) of this subsection is not reached, the legislative process for the draft Statute in the Cortes Generales shall be the same as that for a bill. The text passed by the latter shall be submitted to a referendum of the electorate of the provinces within the territory to be covered by the draft Statute. In the event that it is approved by the majority of validly cast votes in each province, it shall be promulgated as provided in the foregoing paragraph.

3. In the cases described in paragraphs iv) and v) of the foregoing subsection, failure by one or several of the provinces to ratify the draft Statute shall not prevent constitution of the remaining provinces into a Self-governing Community in the manner to be provided for by the organic act contemplated in subsection 1 of this section.

Section 152

1. In the case of Statutes passed by means of the procedure referred to in the foregoing section, the institutional self-government organization shall be based on a Legislative Assembly elected by universal suffrage under a system of proportional representation which shall also assure the representation of the various areas of the territory; an Executive Council with executive and administrative functions and a President elected by the Assembly among its members and appointed by the King. The President shall assume leadership of the Executive Council, the supreme representation of the Community and the State's ordinary representation in the latter. The President and the members of the Executive Council shall be politically accountable to the Assembly.

A High Court of Justice, without prejudice to the jurisdiction of the Supreme Court, shall be the head of Judicial Power in the territory of the Self-governing Community. The Statutes of Autonomy may make provision for the circumstances and the manner in which the Community is to take part in the setting-up of the judicial districts of the territory. Provided that they must conform to the provisions of the Organic Act on the Judicial Power and to the principles of unity and independence of the judicial power.

Without prejudice to the provisions of section 123, successive proceedings, if any, shall be held before judicial bodies located in the same territory of the Self-governing Community in which the Court having jurisdiction in the first instance is located.

2. Once the Statutes have received the Royal Assent and been promulgated, they may be amended only by the procedure provided for therein and a referendum of registered electors in the Self-governing Community.
3. By grouping bordering municipalities together, the Statutes may set up their own territorial constituencies which shall enjoy full legal personality.

Section 153

Control over the bodies of the Self-governing Communities shall be exercised by:

a) The Constitutional Court, in matters pertaining to the constitutionality of their regulatory provisions having the force of law.
b) The Government, after the handing down by the Council of State of its opinion, regarding the exercise of delegated functions referred to in section 150, subsection 2.
c) Jurisdictional bodies of administrative litigation with regard to autonomic administration and its regulations.
d) The Auditing Court, with regard to financial and budgetary matters.

Section 154

A delegate appointed by the Government shall be responsible for the State administration in the territory of each Self-governing Community and shall coordinate it, when necessary, with the Community's own administration.

Section 155

1. If a Self-governing Community does not fulfil the obligations imposed upon it by the Constitution or other laws, or acts in a way that is seriously prejudicial to the general interest of Spain, the Government, after having lodged a complaint with the President of the Self-governing Community and failed to receive satisfaction therefore, may, following approval granted by the overall majority of the Senate, take all measures necessary to compel the Community to meet said obligations, or to protect the abovementioned general interest.
2. With a view to implementing the measures provided for in the foregoing paragraph, the Government may issue instructions to all the authorities of the Self-governing Communities.

Section 156

1. The Self-governing Communities shall enjoy financial autonomy for the development and exercise of their powers, in conformity with the principles of coordination with the State Treasury and solidarity among all Spaniards.

2. The Self-governing Communities may act as delegates or agents of the State for the collection, management and assessment of the latter's tax resources, in conformity with the law and their Statutes.

Section 157

1. The resources of the Self-governing Communities shall consist of:
a) Taxes wholly or partially made over to them by the State; surcharges on State taxes and other shares in State revenue.
b) Their own taxes, rates and special levies.
c) Transfers from an inter-territorial compensation fund and other allocations to be charged to the State Budget.
d) Revenues accruing from their property and private law income.
e) Interest from loan operations.
2. The Self-governing Communities may under no circumstances introduce measures to raise taxes on property located outside their territory or likely to hinder the free movement of goods or services.
3. Exercise of the financial powers set out in subsection 1 above, rules for settling the conflicts which may arise, and possible forms of financial cooperation between the Selfgoverning Communities and the State may be laid down by an organic act.

Section 158

1. An allocation may be made in the State Budget to the Self-governing Communities in proportion to the amount of State services and activities for which they have assumed responsibility and to guarantee a minimum level of basic public services throughout Spanish territory.
2. With the aim of redressing interterritorial economic imbalances and implementing the principle of solidarity, a compensation fund shall be set up for investment expenditure, the resources of which shall be distributed by the Cortes Generales among the Selfgoverning Communities and provinces, as the case may be.

TITULO IX

The Constitutional Court

Section 159

1. The Constitutional Court shall consist of twelve members appointed by the King. Of these, four shall be nominated by the Congress by a majority of three-fifths of its

members, four shall be nominated by the Senate with the same majority, two shall be nominated by the Government, and two by the General Council of the Judicial Power.

2. Members of the Constitutional Court shall be appointed among magistrates and prosecutors, university professors, public officials and lawyers, all of whom must have a recognized standing with at least fifteen years' practice in their profession.

3. Members of the Constitutional Court shall be appointed for a period of nine years and shall be renewed by thirds every three years.

4. Membership of the Constitutional Court is incompatible with any position of a representative nature, any political or administrative office, a management position in a political party or a trade union as well as any employment in their service, active service as a judge or prosecutor and any professional or business activity whatsoever.

Incompatibilities for members of the Judicial Power shall also apply to members of the Constitutional Court.

5. Members of the Constitutional Court shall be independent and enjoy fixity of tenure during their term of office.

Section 160

The President of the Constitutional Court shall be appointed by the King among its members, on the proposal of the full Court itself, for a term of three years.

Section 161

1. The Constitutional Court has jurisdiction over the whole Spanish territory and is entitled to hear:

a) against the alleged unconstitutionality of acts and statutes having the force of an act. A declaration of unconstitutionality of a legal provision having the force of an act and that has already been applied by the Courts, shall also affect the case-law doctrine built up by the latter, but the decisions handed down shall not lose their status of res judicata.

b) Individual appeals for protection (recursos de amparo) against violation of the rights and freedoms contained in section 53(2) of the Constitution, in the circumstances and manner to be laid down by law.

c) Conflicts of jurisdiction between the State and the Self-governing Communities or between the Self-governing Communities themselves.

d) Other matters assigned to it by the Constitution or by organic acts.

2. The Government may appeal to the Constitutional Court against provisions and resolutions adopted by the bodies of the Self-governing Communities, which shall bring about the suspension of the contested provisions or resolutions, but the Court must either ratify or lift the suspension, as the case may be, within a period of not more than five months.

Section 162

1 The following are entitled to:
a) Lodge an appeal of unconstitutionality: the President of the Government, the Defender of the People, fifty Members of Congress, fifty Senators, the Executive body of a Self-governing Community and, where applicable, its Assembly.
b) Lodge an individual appeal for protection (recurso de amparo): any individual or body corporate with a legitimate interest, as well as the Defender of the People and the Public Prosecutor's Office.
2. In all other cases, the organic act shall determine which persons and bodies shall have right of appeal to the Court.

Section 163

If a judicial body considers, when hearing a case, that a regulation having the force of an act which is applicable thereto and upon the validity of which the judgment depends, might be contrary to the Constitution, it may bring the matter before the Constitutional Court in the circumstances, manner and subject to the consequences to be laid down by law, which shall in no case have a suspensive effect.

Section 164

1. The judgments of the Constitutional Court shall be published in the Official State Gazette (Boletín Oficial del Estado), with the dissenting opinions, if any. They have the force of res judicata from the day following their publication, and no appeal may be brought against them. Those declaring the unconstitutionality of an act or of a statute with the force of an act and all those which are not limited to the acknowledgment of an individual right, shall be fully binding on all persons.
2. Unless the judgment rules otherwise, the part of the act not affected by unconstitutionality shall remain in force.

Section 165

An organic act shall make provision for the functioning of the Constitutional Court, the status of its members, the procedure to be followed before it, and the conditions governing actions brought before it.

PART X

Constitutional Amendment

Section 166

The right to propose a constitutional amendment shall be exercised under the provisions of section 87, subsections 1 and 2.

Section 167

1. Bills on constitutional amendments must be approved by a majority of three-fifths of members of each House. If there is no agreement between the Houses, an effort to reach it shall be made by setting up a Joint Committee of an equal number of Members of Congress and Senators which shall submit a text to be voted on by the Congress and the Senate.
2. If approval is not obtained by means of the procedure outlined in the foregoing subsection, and provided that the text has been passed by the overall majority of the members of the Senate, the Congress may pass the amendment by a two-thirds vote in favour.
3. Once the amendment has been passed by the Cortes Generales, it shall be submitted to ratification by referendum, if so requested by one tenth of the members of either House within fifteen days after its passage.

Section 168

1. If a total revision of the Constitution is proposed, or a partial revision thereof, affecting the Introductory Part, Chapter II, Division 1 of Part I, or Part II, the principle of the proposed reform shall be approved by a two-thirds majority of the members of each House, and the Cortes Generales shall immediately be dissolved.
2. The Houses elected thereupon must ratify the decision and proceed to examine the new constitutional text, which must be passed by a two-thirds majority of the members of each House.
3. Once the amendment has been passed by the Cortes Generales, it shall be submitted to ratification by referendum.

Section 169

The process of constitutional amendment may not be initiated in time of war or under any of the states contemplated in section 116.

ADDITIONAL PROVISIONS

One.
The Constitution protects and respects the historic rights of the territories with traditional charts (fueros). The general updating of historic rights shall be carried out, where appropriate, within the framework of the Constitution and of the Statutes of Autonomy.

Two.
The provision of section 12 of this Constitution regarding the coming of age, shall not be prejudicial to cases in which traditional charts are applicable within the sphere of private law.

Three.
Any change in the financial and tax system of the Canary Islands shall require a previous report from the Self-governing Community or, as the case may be, from the provisional selfgovernment body.

Four.
In Self-governing Communities where more than one Court of Appeal (Audiencia Territorial) holds jurisdiction, the Statutes of Autonomy may maintain the existing Courts and share out jurisdiction among them, provided this is done in accordance with the provisions of the Organic Act on the Judicial Power and in conformity with the unity and independence of the latter.

TRANSITIONAL PROVISIONS

One.
In territories with a provisional self-government regime, their higher corporate bodies may, by means of a resolution adopted by the overall majority of their members, assume for themselves the initiative for autonomy which section 143, subsection 2, confers upon the Provincial Councils or corresponding inter-island bodies.

Two.
The territories which in the past have, by plebiscite, approved draft Statutes of Autonomy and which at the time of the promulgation of this Constitution, have provisional self-government regimes, may proceed immediately in the manner contemplated in section 148, subsection 2, if agreement to do so is reached by the overall majority of their pre self-government higher corporate bodies, and the Government shall be duly informed. The draft Statutes shall be drawn up in

accordance with the provisions of section 151, subsection 2, where so requested by the pre Self-government assembly.

Three.
The right to initiate the process towards self-government conferred on local authorities or their members, provided in section 143, subsection 2, shall be postponed for all purposes until the first local elections have taken place, once the Constitution has come into force.

Four.
1. In the case of Navarra, and for the purpose of its integration into the General Basque Council or into the autonomous Basque institutions which may replace it, the procedure contemplated by section 143 of this Constitution shall not apply. The initiative shall lie instead with the appropriate historic institution (órgano foral), whose decision must be taken by the majority of its members. The initiative shall further require for its validity the ratification by a referendum expressly held to this end and approval by the majority of votes validly cast.
2. If the initiative does not succeed, it may only be repeated during a further term of office of the competent Foral body and, in any case, after the minimum period laid down in section 143 has elapsed.

Five.
The cities of Ceuta and Melilla may set themselves up as Self-governing Communities if their respective City Councils so decide in a resolution adopted by the overall majority of their members and if the Cortes Generales so authorize them by an organic act, under section 144.

Six.
Where several draft Statutes are referred to the Constitutional Committee of the Congress, they shall be considered in the order in which they are received. The two month period referred to in section 151 shall be counted from the moment in which the Committee completes its study of the draft or of the drafts that it has successively examined.

Seven.
The provisional self-government bodies shall be considered to be dissolved in the following cases:
a) Once the bodies provided for by the Statutes of Autonomy passed in conformity with the Constitution have been set up.
b) In the event that the initiative for the obtention of autonomy status should not be successful for non-compliance with the requirements of section 143.
c) If the relevant body has not exercised the right recognized in the First Transitional Provision within a period of three years.

Eight.

1. Once the present Constitution has come into force, the Houses that have adopted it shall assume the functions and powers set out therein for the Congress and the Senate respectively. Provided that under no circumstances shall their term of office continue beyond June 15, 1981.

2. With regard to the provisions of section 99, the promulgation of the Constitution shall be considered as creating the constitutional basis for the subsequent application of those provisions. To this end, there shall be a thirty day period, as from the date of the promulgation, for implementing the provisions contained in said section.

During this period, the current President of the Government assuming the functions and powers vested by the Constitution for this office, may decide to use the authority conferred by section 115 or, through resignation, leave the way open for application of section 99. In the latter case, the situation as regards the President shall be that provided in subsection 2 of section 101.

3. In the event of dissolution, in accordance with section 115, and if the provisions contained in sections 68 and 69 have not been enacted, the rules previously in force shall apply to the ensueing elections, except for causes of ineligibility and incompatibilities, to which section 70, subsection 1, paragraph b), of this Constitution shall be directly applicable, as well as its provisions concerning voting age and those of ection 69, subsection 3.

Nine.

Three years after the election of the members of the Constitutional Court of the first tie, lots shall be drawn to choose a group of four members of the same electoral origin who are to resign and be replaced. The two members appointed following proposal by the Government and the two appointed following proposal by the General Council of the Judicial Power shall be considered as members of the same electoral origin exclusively for this purpose. After three years have elapsed, the same procedure shall be carried out with regard to the two groups not affected by the aforementioned drawing of lots. Thereafter, the provisions contained in subsection 3 of section 159 shall apply.

REPEALS

1. Act 1/1977, of January 4, for Political Reform, is hereby repealed, as well as the following, in so far as they were not already repealed by the above-mentioned Act: the Act of the Fundamental Principles of National Movement of May 17, 1958; the Chart of the Spanish People (Fuero de los Españoles) of July 17, 1945; the Labour Chart of March 9, 1938; the Act of Constitution of the Cortes of July 17, 1942; the Act of Succession to the Head of State of July 26, 1947, all of them as amended by the Organic Act of the State of January 10, 1967. The last mentioned Act and that of the National Referendum of October 22, 1945, are likewise repealed.

2. To the extent that it may still retain some validity, the Act of October 25, 1839 shall be definitively repealed in so far as it applies to the provinces of Alava, Guipúzcoa and Vizcaya.
Subject to the same terms, the Act of July 21, 1876 shall be deemed to be definitively repealed.
3. Likewise, any provisions contrary to those contained in the Constitution are hereby repealed.

FINAL PROVISION

This Constitution shall come into force on the day of publication of its official text in the Official State Gazette (Boletín Oficial del Estado). It shall also be published in the other languages of Spain.

WHEREFORE,
WE ORDER ALL SPANIARDS, WHETHER INDIVIDUALS OR AUTHORITIES, TO ABIDE BY THIS CONSTITUTION AND ENSURE THAT IT IS OBSERVED AS A FUNDAMENTAL LAW OF THE STATE.
PALACIO DE LAS CORTES, THE TWENTY-SEVENTH OF DECEMBER OF NINETEEN HUNDRED AND SEVENTY-EIGTH.

JUAN CARLOS

THE PRESIDENT OF THE CORTES
Antonio Hernández Gil

THE SPEAKER OF THE CONGRESS
Fernando Alvarez de Miranda y Torres

THE SPEAKER OF THE SENATE
Antonio Fontán Pérez

www.ingramcontent.com/pod-product-compliance
Lightning Source LLC
Chambersburg PA
CBHW031550210526
45464CB00003B/1233